JOHNNY CASH - AMERICAN V:
A Hundred Highways

ISBN 13: 978-1-4234-1988-4
ISBN 10: 1-4234-1988-X

HAL•LEONARD®
CORPORATION
7777 W. BLUEMOUND RD. P.O. BOX 13819 MILWAUKEE, WI 53213

Visit Hal Leonard Online at
www.halleonard.com

JOHNNY CASH - AMERICAN V:
A Hundred Highways

4   HELP ME

10   GOD'S GONNA CUT YOU DOWN

17   LIKE THE 309

26   IF YOU COULD READ MY MIND

33   FURTHER ON UP THE ROAD

39   ON THE EVENING TRAIN

43   I CAME TO BELIEVE

49   LOVE'S BEEN GOOD TO ME

53   A LEGEND IN MY TIME

58   ROSE OF MY HEART

61   FOUR STRONG WINDS

67   I'M FREE FROM THE CHAIN GANG NOW

HELP ME

Words and Music by
LARRY GATLIN

Moderately fast

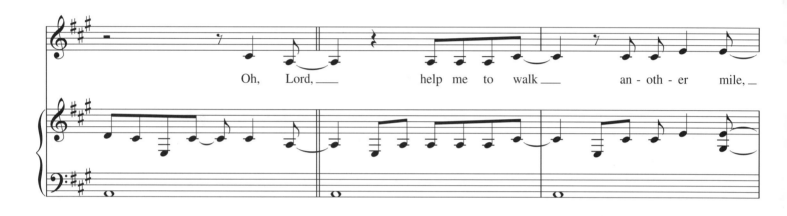

Oh, Lord, ___ help me to walk ___ an - oth - er mile, ___

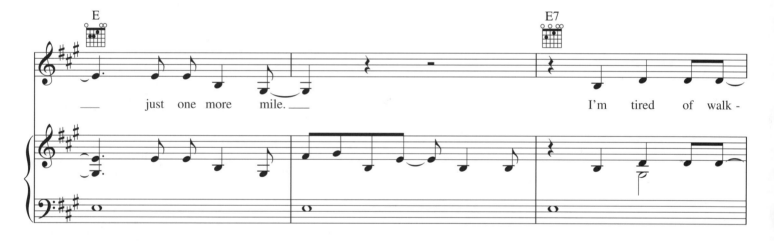

___ just one more mile. ___ I'm tired of walk-

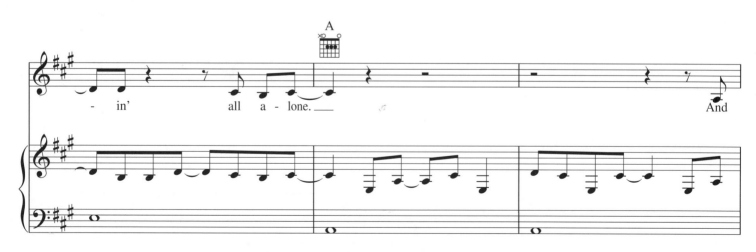

-in' all a - lone. ___ And

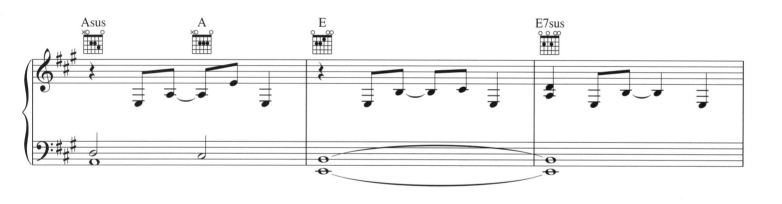

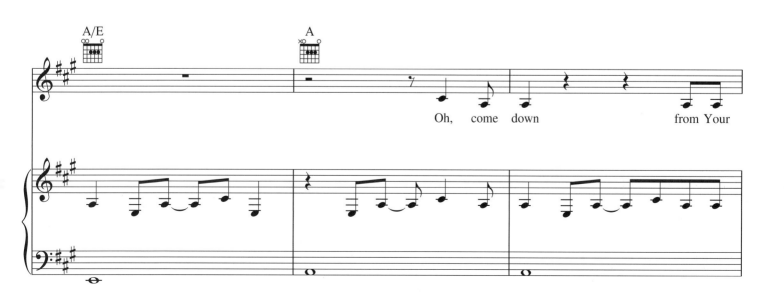

Oh, come down from Your

D.S. al Coda

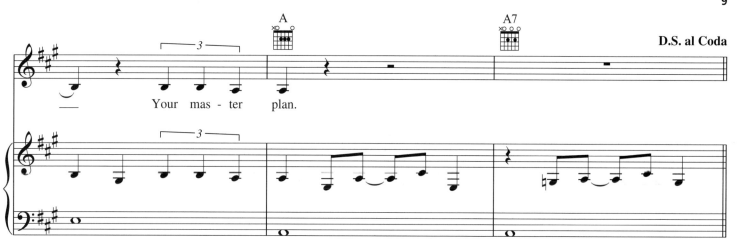

Your mas - ter plan.

CODA

With a hum - ble heart, on bend - ed knee, ____

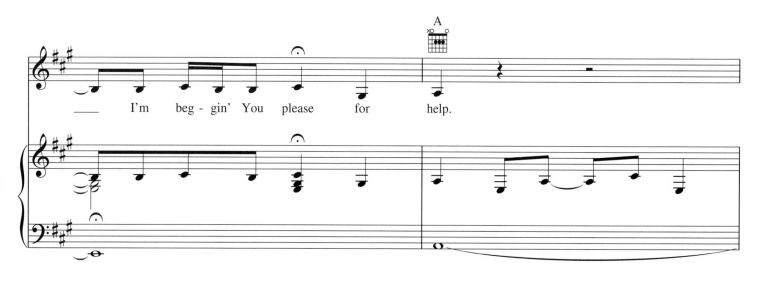

____ I'm beg - gin' You please for help.

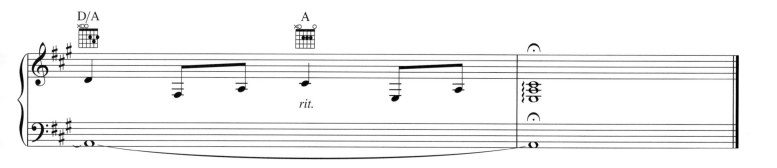

rit.

GOD'S GONNA CUT YOU DOWN

Traditional
Arranged by JOHN R. CASH

LIKE THE 309

Written by
JOHN R. CASH

It should be a - while __ be - fore I see Doc - tor Death, __ so it would

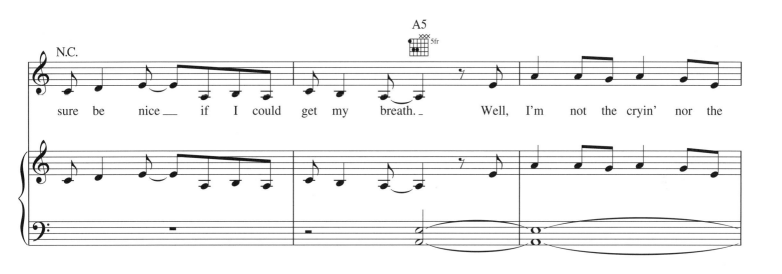

sure be nice __ if I could get my breath. __ Well, I'm not the cryin' nor the

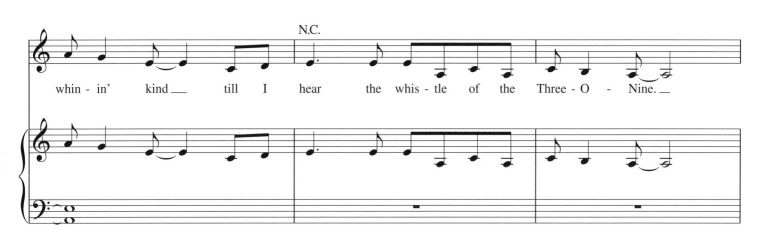

whin - in' kind __ till I hear the whis - tle of the Three - O - Nine. __

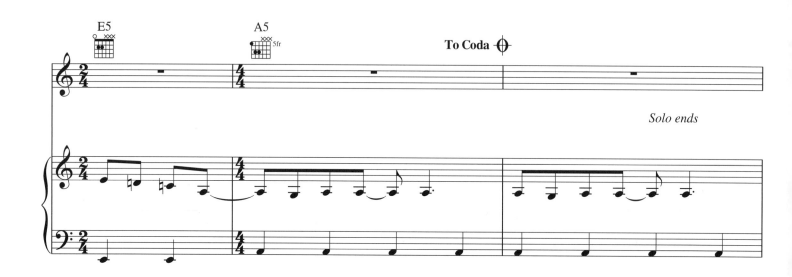

IF YOU COULD READ MY MIND

Words and Music by
GORDON LIGHTFOOT

feel-ing's gone __ and I just can't get it back. __

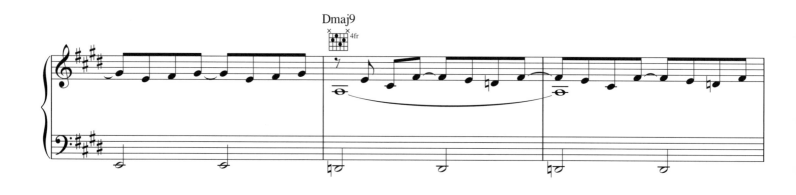

poco rit.

FURTHER ON
(Up the Road)

Words and Music by
BRUCE SPRINGSTEEN

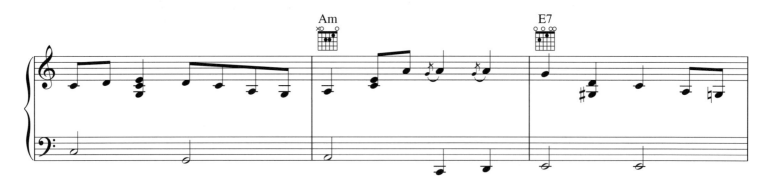

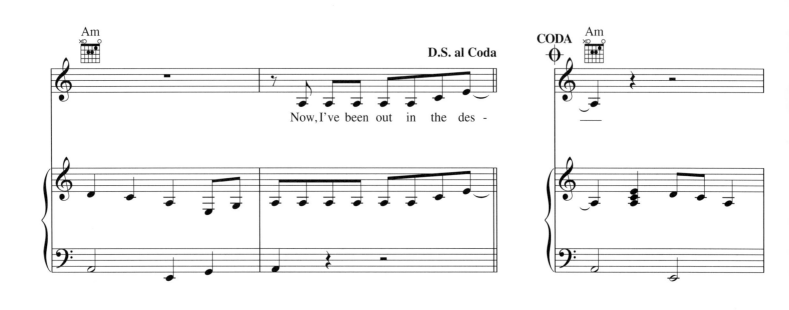

D.S. al Coda

Now, I've been out in the des -

CODA

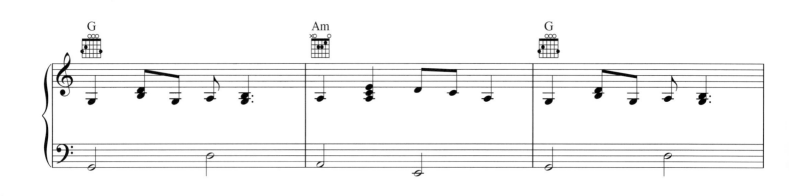

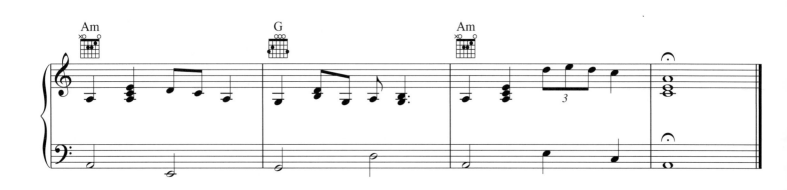

ON THE EVENING TRAIN

Words and Music by HANK WILLIAMS
and AUDREY WILLIAMS

I heard the

laugh-ter at the de - pot, but my tears fell like the
_____ a-way from the de - pot, it seemed I heard her call my

I CAME TO BELIEVE

Written by
JOHN R. CASH

I could - n't
Noth - in' worked

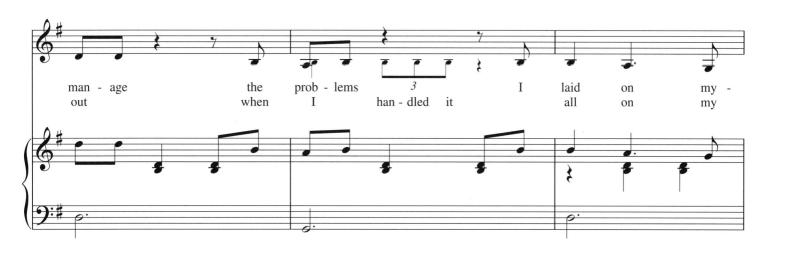

man - age   the prob - lems   I   laid   on   my -
out   when I han - dled it   all   on   my

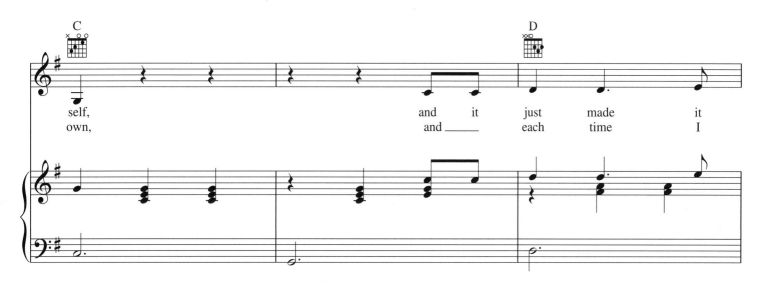

self,   and it   just made   it
own,   and ____ each time   I

lieve   in a pow - er   much high - er   than

LOVE'S BEEN GOOD TO ME

Words and Music by
ROD McKUEN

To Coda

(I'd Be)
A LEGEND IN MY TIME

Words and Music by
DON GIBSON

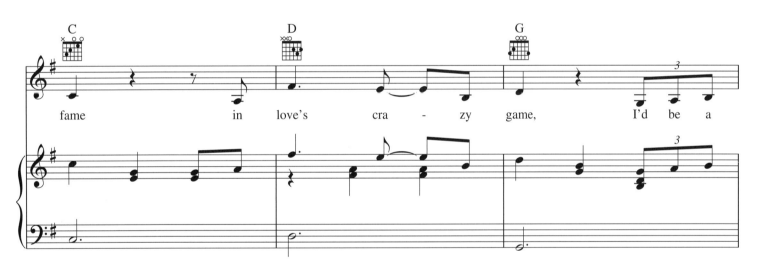

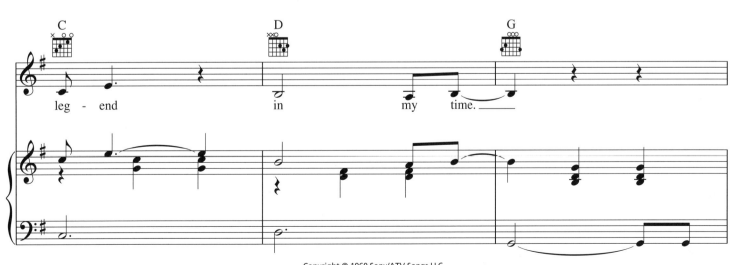

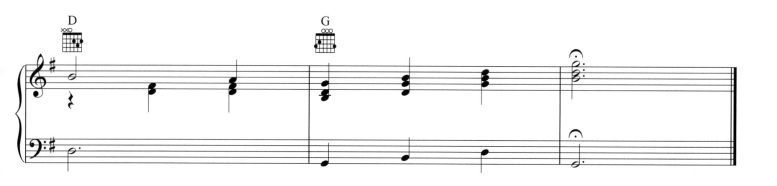

ROSE OF MY HEART

Words and Music by
HUGH MOFFATT

FOUR STRONG WINDS

Words and Music by
IAN TYSON

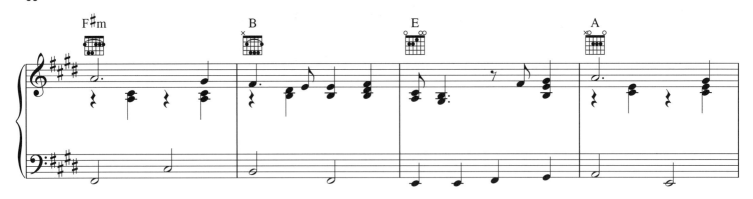

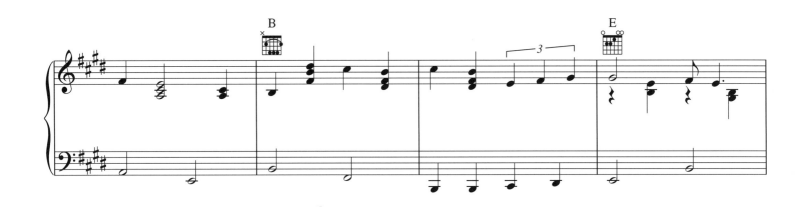

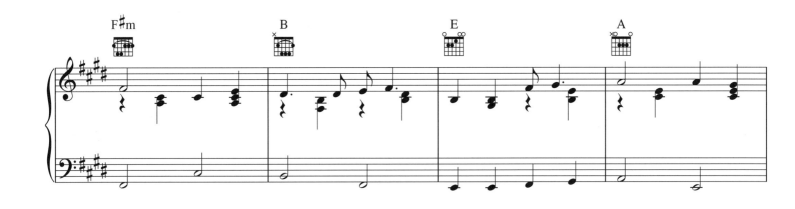

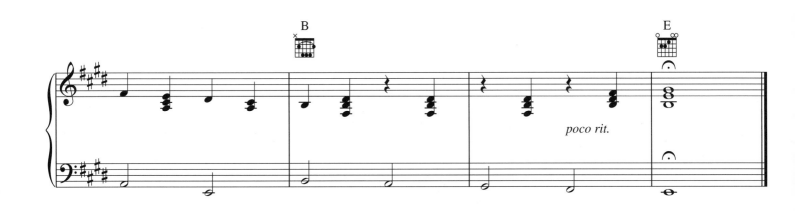

I'M FREE FROM THE CHAIN GANG NOW

Words and Music by LOU HERSCHER
and SAUL KLEIN